This book was published by Stewed Rhubarb Press
in May 2019, with the ISBN number
978-1-910416-07-5

Typesetting, layout and cover by
James T. Harding
www.james-t-harding.com

THIS SCRIPT

JENNY LINDSAY

www.stewedrhubarb.org

In memory of
Isabel Lindsay (1932 – 2017)
and
Jean Finlayson (1931 – 2018)

Contents

A Margin of Error

You, solitary reader,
have often terrified
me with your
distance.
Cannae see the whites
of yer eyes – nor
your boredom,
feel your laughter.
Not a chance of
that nice *mmnnnnhmm*
poetry-audience noise neither.
As a *performance poet*, obviously
I
am a craver of attention,
applause, post-gig analysis, the banter –
and here, there cannae be a *Hello!*
How are ye?
which is how I like to start
conversations with strangers
which this very is.

> (It is rather)

But black wi white is a
different game
to crafting sound wi silence, so –
let the margin be my feet:
steady, holding this thing together;

> (I may skedaddle)

let line breaks be
breath
or pause or pulse or
sometimes, mibbes,
a wee bit arbitrary, for
it's only natural
that ye shuffle a bit

when yer nervous,
about to tell a total ran
dom a pure bucket
load of everything...

This script is fu
ae bloody forms and
squelching marshy wanderings.
Walking here tonight
I passed three skeletons,
over eighty frogs,
two rapists,
had much voluntary but unwanted sex,
two hundred and forty menstrual cycles,
met several mentors,
tipped my hat
to the realisation that
100% of all idols are
at least 80% arsehole.

Solitary judgement.

But here we are, at any rate,
in this room/café/bed/pub/bath-tub
                              (delete as appropriate)
with the black wi white
and the sound wi silence
burbling with whatever that is
in the background.
                              (insert your own soundtrack)

It's really nice to meet you – *Hello!* –
or to see you again, whichever fits – *How are ye?*
I'm Jenny,
Jenny Lindsay, aye,
and
this is
This Script.

Fuck You Tuesday

seagulls screech like stabbed cats
alarm bells thud hearts tae waken
my own cat chirp-chirps fir bisquits

oh fuck me sideways
this mortal lurch
from bed to kitchen to
shower to gag

last night was Fuck You Tuesday
a lover and i's occasional ritual –
a ritual as unlikely as our coupling –
age-old set up
Younger Poet meets
let's call em
Older Biologist

and wine is sunk
and cards are thumped
firmly on the table
as they were many years ago
i'm technically old too now, i suggest
he harrumphs at this
quite rightly

he's a biologist
i know not his world
and he has very little time
for poetry in performance
but Fuck You Tuesday
is less an ego stroke –
and in fact the Fuck You is
aimed squarely at the weekday –
we're both just thirsty
and free
nae ego-stroke here, nope,
more a

jesus christ! what a calamity!
this helluva world! this
helluva art – nae substance and
nae fuck you to direct it at, directly – acht!

our love's made of frantic
and all of a sudden
both wanting a fuck of
youth and wisdom
simultaneously
and paracetamol
eventually...

Fuck You Tuesday:
an irregular relief
a thrusty cum and
for me, some solace
in my rented room
i awake to a note
on the desk every time –

sometimes loving
sometimes arbitrary
sometimes nothing

tuesday is ours to fuck with
but we're careful to
never let it spill
intae overtime

Jenny's Let Herself Go

Jenny's let herself go
the snippy chitter of a thrip
heard across an ocean
Jenny's let herself go – mirror,
i chose this, in dough
malbec   masturbation   smoke
Jenny's let herself go
if even he cannot love it
with all he knows – spiral –
Jenny's let herself go
a mother's flitting disapproval
at ordering mighty
club sandwiches
Jenny's let herself go
fuck this scene shit poet ego
no money   self-indulgence
Jenny's let herself go
i *know*   I KNOW   i know
i know   *i* know
Jenny's let herself go
into a sleepless hermit cave
with an orgy of policemen manning
Jenny's going to let
her liver burn and explode
under baggier clothes
Jenny's let herself go
I wonder where any of her parts
might survive the letting that
Jenny's going to explore before
she gets the better
of inside
beside herself

Gender Me
a dance in 'E' and 'O'

gender me   endlessly
tell me be she meekly
keep shht be sweet
never depress menz feelz
centre them endlessly

gender me   sexy
few extremes exempt here
send me sex texts
bend me endlessly
       he
knees

            eyes
deplete cheeks
clench (HERE)   flex (HERE)
beeeeeeeeend
(schexy.....)
eek

gender me genteel
prevent self-serve   deter depth
get me green-eyed   wetten me
green-eyed   weep weep weep

stew me sleek   speck her speech

extreme gender sends he-men helter-skelter
she – endlessly lesser   feeble
gender blend these messes sweet

keep me femme fresh
helpless shell   blended essence present
(remember self-esteem!)

gender blend served
gender blend serves

serves who well?

well?

Go on. Chop chop.
Who storms to top jobs?
strong-hold from shop floor to prof?
pooh-poohs non-conform *trollops*?
spoons orthodox plonk on wombs?
Top dog throng   odds on not
snowdrops or sows...
No: strong wolf.
Pomp-pomp old-school plots for now:
from Good Book to cold blood,
common rooms to crowds.
From boy to dog's bollocks boss who
holds jobs for so-so boys,
scorns good work from dolls;
prowls   swoons   drools
on hot-blossom bosoms
looks down on old for   no worth, hm?
No.

Doll! Don't confront too gobby – no!
Go coo. Comfort, don't confront!
Crooks don't go down – dolls do!
Thrown down.

Don't   we   ?

Gender me   secrets kept restlessly
Then
#MeToo
Two word, two vowel combo

More power to elbows.

The Schism Ring

There Will Be Cake!
at the feminist literary gathering –
and *tea and biscuits!* and
gluten-free and vegan options!
exclamatory sprinkles and
safety warnings and
in-case-of-fire announcements
and Formica tables
and ghastly lighting
and a recognition and
a *catering for everybody*
covered and
uncovered by all topics listed.

Sometimes
 – and I admit this
in full knowledge of
all the ways it is
problematic –
I want a banquet of frogs' legs,
duck eggs and steak;
piles of mashed potatoes laden
with full-fat butter and bacon
 – the setting a dimly lit, cavernous hall –
flagons of ridiculously expensive
craft ales that we've chored
from some dickhead bar

and I wish for a
big fuck-off boxing ring
 – non-lethal, fully accessible[*] –
designed for pillow fights
to sort out our differences.
We'll call it
The Schism Ring
and, just as now,
a match will be declared

and who cares who wins?
because
afterwards, we'll devour chicken wings
and mozzarella buns
smothered in the hottest of hot sauce,
get merry on bottles of malbec,
and shout
FUCK YOUR BIOLOGICAL ESSENTIALISM!
                    FUCK YOUR GENDER ESSENTIALISM!
And then we'll hug
with these bodies – different
chests and breasts squishing
together in at least tacit understanding,
if not love.
And then we'll go dancing:
belly dancing!
limbo! fire! jazz! daftie!
And we'll be too full up for
baking...

Oh, folks, are we not bored of
angry Twitter sneers
and bigot calls
and hatred assumptions?
Tired of pouty faux-doe selfies
and lollipops and
'Fuck The Patriarchy' tote bags,
and manicured, manufactured
resistance?

Women under thirty calling
their older sisters irrelevant witches
after all that they have done for us
IS MAKING ME VERY HUNGRY
for a family feast of reconciliation
 – not agreement, nope –
a hearty banquet though,
not a polite, wee, agreeable cupcake.

Oh! You reckon this is too *masculine*
as I devour meat on the bone with bare hands?
I will not use cutlery or wipe my face silent when
I am judged by other criteria from men.
I'll fail no tick-box exercise in purity –
demure purity is
the wrong ingredient
unless we're wanting
egged face,
sunk flans,
cakes deflated,
in the kitchen.

So bring your lemon drizzle,
your rocky road,
your red velvet.
Bring your banana bread
and marshmallows.
And please do – please do
call me a misogynist.
This verse is dripping
with their damn stuff.
It's very calorific
and I am one – at times –
and so are you, because
we're fighting a system we are part of,
not individual atoms.

So bring your ripened, arrogant plum puds,
your nippy wee ginger biscuits,
your thirsty tongues,
your razor wit sliced intae sixes
by all things listed.
Bring fistfuls of chocolate-cookie crust
and melting, childhood strawberry ices.

Bring your loathing
– self and otherwise.
Bring your love.

Bring your love.

---

* The Schism Ring is also open to food fights and most importantly –
all are welcome.

11

Bookmarked

A feeling of absence
even before you're gone...
The clichés form
in the back of my mind as
the room cools to morning.

I know this script.
I know these lessons
but I never memorise them.
There is a gluttony in this revision.

You
are
a bullet-point
list
of
things
I should tick off as done and been there.
Highlight ye off in
pink, slick, done.

But there is a gluttony
in re-reading passages
already fingered, thumbed.

Penned in your margins
I imagine my name is scored:
a note to self to revise this text again,
perhaps find a secondary meaning,

or, alternatively, at least something nourishing...
breakfast?

Sure. I could drawer ye,
file you away as an uncompleted work,
waste more time.
And yet, I don't.

You don't even know if you are novel,
poem, song, *BuzzFeed* article...

I don't know if I am reader
or author – you as character,
me as god?

We are postmodern, are we?
Playful but pointless.
A bookmark tumbling from pages
blanking themselves, falling down
the back of my bed,
only ever mine, after all.

Maybe it's still there,
gathering dust and crumbs?
I don't want it back, of course.

You don't know
what you want, I tell myself,
and though I do not know why
I would even want this,
I bookmark the
possibility in the air
as your naked back
becomes shirted.

And it Dawns on Me

all the hypochondriacs I know, including myself
are heavy escapists, smokers and drinkers
heavy aware of inevitability

undiagnosed, terminal, full of certainty
they visit no doctors but regularly
write their own obituaries.

An Invite
to Your Baby Shower or Your Child's Birthday Party

They don't make them like they used to.
Don't make women like yer Gran did.
Nor daughter's like yer Ma did.
Or girls like this absence
in the shape of a child.

I'll send best wishes. Maybe
1 might come sip
awkward prosecco at the barbie,
get accidentally pished like
my 'aunties' did.

But never ask me of ideal worlds,
or if this choice is choice,
or look at me knowingly when
you hear I'm in love now –
there is no path but the one that's walked.

This *Hello, welcome to the world! I wish you wonder!*
Joy! Nae Larkin!
is all 1 have to give at present.
This cradled hope, though
no gifts were asked for,
no gifts demanded.

Have a Kid

Have a kid and be judged cos yer sixteen
Have a kid and be judged cos yer thirty-five
Have a kid and be judged cos yer out of work and can't
vitamin up yer kid and take em to karate, ballet, posh
    school, Laser Quest, pony rides, Dominos lunch with pals

Have a kid and vegan em deficient in nutrients
Have a kid and carnivore em intae game play
Have a kid and hate them
Have a kid and love them til the balloon bursts
Have a kid and show them *Bambi*, buy donuts and hate
    yerself when you eat them

Have a kid and try whatever the week throws at ye
Have a kid and dream in pillowed temporary solace
Have a kid and have em cute in a ball pool
Have a kid and inject caffeine in yer temple
Have a kid and resent yer loss of work due to working
    ovaries and a lucky sperm that squiggles scot-free from
    all responsibilities, but not casting calls

For some reason that sperm is like a black dot against your
name in the listings, while its owner gets to hear applause for
occasionally taking a selfie and smiling like they give it their
all in a fucken sand box with the kid that bears your surname
and primary-carer status assigned to yerself, though *it's all
equal, aye, it's all equal* – he's dating, you're not – cos you had a
kid, didn't ye, and who wants that? He couldn't be arsed with
the you that you had to become because you had to because
you agreed to

Have a kid and nourish them with all of your kindness
Have a kid and fill them with the love that you lacked
Have a kid and never, ever abandon them
Have a kid and defy the Philip fucking Larkin verse

Have a kid cos it's none of their business
Have a kid because it is none of mine
Don't have a kid
for exactly the same reasons

and let's be less judgey, shall we, on both sides?

The Heart of the House

Let them call our bodies haunted houses
where the ghosts never actually lived at all

Let them call us barren
husks   flushed tombs
Gardens become graveyards, they sing
in the absence of our spurts
and our sprucings

You need stronger foundations,
perhaps a fountain, they trill
suggesting improvements
those amateur interior designers
with the wrong tools

This complex, delicate structure
will liquefy and bloat
Putrefied lungs will not
be sparked back tae life
no matter how good
their electricians.

And as they fill our spaces with their ideas
they will tell us to *have no fear* –
despite the bodies they've left
in our basements, and the boots,
the muddied, bloodied boots everywhere

Let them
Let them

Let them rebuild us in
their image of perfection:
mibbes a flashy play mansion
or 50s sink-chained pleasant
backlash angels mounted
in the entrance hall

frilly gingham kitchen
bleached lawn
shaved hillock
plucked splinters

Let them comment on our handles
Let them rip down the monthly cleansing rota –
call it outdated   surplus to requirements
Let them misunderstand how
this house breathes a sigh of relief
at the order of our ageing facilities
Let them *never mind* it
Let them take it away
steam out our nether bows

Let them make us ghosts in our own haunted houses
Let them market us as *in need of a re-fit*
too old for selling for a premium as is –
who would buy *this* through desire alone?
A project, that's how you sell this one, brothers
Drape some fairy lights around the backlash angels
Trim the wings tae genteel

And now promote us in an advertising brochure
with a squeaky clean plasticky *mmm* overtone
and a picture of the facade from a decade ago

Let them
Let them

Witches   spinsters   batshitmadams   harridans
ladies   bitches   women   the heart of the house

We will not rest
We will not cease
We are all we are
We are all we ever were
And some will miss us

This Machine

...but then it hits me like a hot-iron thump tae the chest that maims and sticks and pulls away at the flesh that... shit. This is all there is. So why then hasten the end with this quickening towards nothingness? Drinking it, smoking it, washing it down with sugared tar? Why – because the alternatives are so boring? Because I cannae make that logic stick? Every inch of 'me' protests the new meaning of what This is. This Script. This Thing. This brick, smashing the mirror before asking what the point is. This script insists there is no link between the sense of self and the fleshy machine I carry it around in. Agreed. There is no link. Because they are of one, surely? This is the package. It is. Isn't it? And this machine engages in the small pleasures that harm it as if it were not. As if some *self* or *soul* transcended it.

This is embarrassing.
As is the alternative.

The Imagined We

We are never permitted to be human
poets, writers, journalists, whatevers
We are female poets. Women
writers. We are murdered women
We are statistics
We are problems to be solved
We are problems to be represented

Each of the imagined we who rises up
becomes us, whether we like it or not

Do not tear them down, sisters!
Do not tear us down, women folk!

It is not womanly *of us, to us*
to be at each other's throats

not when they are our throats

not when sirens are the soundtrack tae our newsfeeds

or, we are slashed at the throat
We are severed heads weighed down with rocks
in bin bags chucked far from our bodies
our humanity shucked off
by default humans' hands

We stand in the shower
The blood trickles down our thighs on
One of *those* days
One of *those* days
One of those days
Where we're encouraged
Me time!
Me *time!*
ME TIME!

Alone with *chocolate!*
Alone with scrummy bubble-baths in delicious flavours!

Misogyny Mud-pie and Mint?
Creamy Dreamy Cum-dumpster Froth!
Raspberry Coulis and Kool-Aid? *Mmm!*
Paedo Pear with Jojoba and Argan Oil?
Lollipop…

We plug it in all holes, don't we?

We lean our heads on the tiles and
watch our blood plop and pool
because the plug-hole is blocked.

We imagine that an epic car-chase
followed by fist fights led us here to
this bleeding from a hidden wound –
and that we are renegades! We are superheroes!
                                   (or perhaps functioning drunk
                                        anti-heroes)
We have trauma in our pasts and we are
Setting Things Right!

The Imagined THEM! The bad guys
have been left in pools of writhing regret!
Some of them have stakes sticking out of where
their hearts once were – some of them
turned tae dust in front of our eyes.

And we are bruised
We are injured
But we are alive

We are just temporarily crunched over
tenderised, bleeding from the fight

This script writes itself
Plop
      plop
              plops
In our silence...

PICTURE THE SCENE:

Strings rise up
are soon accompanied by brass
as the camera angle switches
from our point of view
It starts at polished toe-nails that
sparkle through our bloodied feet
pans up smoothly – at the same speed
as that constant little trickle
The lens ensures a glimpse
of our shaved mound
There's a sloooo
ooowing at un-suckled nipple

And then, our face
our face in tight-lipped defiance
closed-eyed anger
and then a sudden SNAPPING OPEN!
Clearly, fierce pain inside

The scene ends with our fists
punching and then
pummelling the tiles
our strangled throats expleting
our knuckles bloodied too now
all this fucking PAIN!

At which an audience will cry:

BRAVO!

What fighting spirit!

Triumph over adversity!

All those banished demons!

and the removal of awards.

Rewards limited tae a fist
smashing another fist
and being told it's the fights against us
that make us who we are?

And that we must love the pain of this at all costs.

We must love the pain of this at all costs.

This Script
a part-univocal poem in and about 'I'

Since six, it imprints in skin –
this girl script, this birthright which kills spirit.
Whilst timid lips twitch *Shhhhh, girls*
swirl mildly within this
is itch in this skin, in this script

Misfits spit:
KILL THIS!
Whip nit-wits stingingly with livid riffs!
This script stinks!
It is shirt lifts. It is skirt shims with impish grins
It is slits pink, bikini tits. It is
pricks infringing with victim scripts
It is in birth til infirm
this script, this girlish mimicry...

Grim risk if girls wish trim bits within knicks!
If thigh-ripping thick skins in big biffs shirts
bits binding within rigid distinct ticks ID-ing with
script-ish wish-lists is inspiring?   PFT!
It binds 'I' within slim-picking piddling limits!

Misfits flick digits. Fists twitch. Indignity fizzing.
Sighs rising.

I
GIRL
Is it implicit? Is it ID?
This insipid script – is it simply right?
Writ in birth?   Identity?   Cis?

                              (is this msprnt??)

Kick it. Stick it in bins brimming with skin flicks!
High-five other 'I's!
Let a collective 'I' light up within winning shin-kickings!
Bitches, reclaim this script!
Be singing: one is not born, one becomes WOMAN!

                          oops...   off script...

It's illicit thinking, skirting kinship with siblings whilst
hissing indignity within isms splits ID from 'I's –
Schisms rip Twit'ring vigils
Timid girls flit, sighing:
Skirmish! Irk! Pitching in is visibility! Crisis-rid!

Shhhhh
Shhhhh

Kick it. This script?
It's 'I' ridden
'I' is limiting
'I' is 'I' first
Tight-knit wiring gives wind chill

We are not this script
Though we act it well – and with vim
'I' stands still, individual,
while a collective head wricks necks tae listen.

How to Be a Stalker

He said: You are a beautifully souled car crash of a woman
I want to save and adore and own.

He said: You hurt my feelings last night, you little bitch.
Stop playing games with me, you know
we were meant to be together...

He said: I know you could call the police on me again,
but I'm banking that you're not so cruel...

He said: You are disgusting,
you man-hating whore.
You will be with cats forever.

He said: You will die alone.

Feminism Meets Capitalism for a Dram

I'm here
because you asked me politely.
You were persuasive.
And clever
to make it seem like my choice.

But don't think for a second
that I don't know what yer up to.
We've been doing this dance
for years now after-all.
Yes. I saw
the 'This Is What A Feminist Looks Like'
t-shirt marketing campaign.
And those Dove adverts – nice one.
Grudgingly, I see what you did there,
chum.

But the
touchable fuckable rapeable cunting sub
ject of this is
still unknown to ye.

And my tongue is a dumb slug trying to sip
this pink drink you've ordered me –
I thought we were meeting for a dram?

Aye, I know that the ladette
marketing campaign is now
so yester-century,
and yer keener now on the
simpering-pretty-box tick
and the strong-and-androgynous box tick
and the boxy-tick boxy tick
you're such an individual boxy tick.
But to be quite frank, pal,
I'm not so sure
that's going to stick.

Because the
touchable fuckable rapeable cunting sub
ject of this is
still unknown to ye.

Though, yes, on the surface,
these choices ye offer are gey pretty...

But the
touchable fuckable rapeable cunting sub
ject of this is
still unknown to ye.

Though... I want this so very much.
I want to be beautiful.
I want to be loved.

I want to want you but not want you later,
want to want you but not be wanted back,
want you to want me but not know I might need ye.

Cos this is crap, pal, it is crap –
and I know
and you know
and I know

that I will take you home tonight
and I will fuck you
like there's cameras.
And yet our bodies?
They'll not converse.

Because the
touchable fuckable rapeable cunting sub
ject of this is
still unknown to ye.

Listen, you know this,
you knew this before you
even invited me here to this bar!
You've known me for years.

You know how I have known
the panting ache of another's absence,
the splits and the schisms
that have ripped at my heart,
and I have longed for the tangy wrap
of familiarity in a shared bed –
though special and separate,
our limbs all intersecting
to one fine and beautiful mess
of hope! Of liberation!

But I find myself forgetting this now,
with my damp, dumb tongue
and the increasing solitude
that you made for me.

With a caged heart so cautious
to beat its truth
it is now breaking itself.

I have paid you with
my fangs,
my love,
my body,
my language,
my time.

And cleverly?
You made it seem like my choice.

But the
touchable fuckable rapeable cunting sub
ject of this is still
unknown to ye.

So, I think it's only fair
that tonight
it's your round,
my gentleman.

Porn is

to sex what
parkour is to
walking down the street

PornHub

In the comments on PornHub
underneath a threesome scene
where
'Two Athletic Sluts Enjoy One Massive Cock':

> *Is it just me... or see compared with her other work?*
> *In this, doesn't she look so much better without make-up?*

> *He goes flaccid at 31 minutes in. I think that's*
> *really disrespectful.*

> *The basketball, though? I did find that*
> *a little distracting...*

Plural anal prolapse bud
painful blossoms on their screens.
The headless thruster keeps his socks on

mise en scène.

Backlash at a Bar
a scene in 'A'

At a bar, an alpha-man awayday.
Brawn and banal chat blasts at all.
Cat-calls catch at jaws that call back
   Last straw, lads! Hashtag, ALL lads... Arg...
Walk past. Walk past a backlash pack.

Hard and fast jabs lash at backs –
SCRATCH THAT! THAT TALK-BACK SPRAY!
Backlash? Ah, lads! Warpath!

Ah say: *Man pals –*
lads gawp at carnal acts. Gasp at gaffa gags and
grab and smash; grasp and wank as anal gaps
jam-pack man shafts and jar jaws fast as
gals gag as gals gag as gals gaga as madman
slaps ass and chaps swarm snatch...

And that – and THAT, at a bar – that's a small part,
a backlash at all past laws that...

   Backlash? Man pal spams.
  Nah! Valhalla! adds Dan

What? What? WHAT??   *smack*

A braggart man pal brays, 'FACTS',
grasps tankard, brags:
   Shag as ART. Acht, lass, halt flak at natal brawn!
   Cat-calls, ass slaps? Damn brash... alas FACTS say
   harks back at grassland man.

Backwards bastard, ay? Twat vandals? ah spat.

   Backwards and backlash? Nah! Blatant barb!
   Man as bad alpha – yawn!
   Blank barbs, lass.

Acht...

All lad pals say, *Ahm an ally, lass!*
Back clap, back clap, *Awwww bad man, bad...*
Alas, small jabs add angst day and days and days and
    and

                  flashback   park   ramp   attack
                                          can't can't can't

And chaps *can* chalk attacks as small fracas,
dab hands at gallant placards at a march. Alas
lads canna fash at all acts that rap lack at gal pals –
what scant thanks
what scant warmth
what day and days and days and days and

   backlash   ay man
              flashback   park   ramp   attack
can't
can't
can't

// this script this birth-right which kills spirit kick it stick it in bins brimming with the skin-flick pornos they're licking their lips at this skin ripping insisting in him hinting it's fine hinting it's natural hinting it's normal and you're a bitch nasty feminist nasty woman who wants to shin-kick for no reason

Also. Goddammit, Jenny, ma pal...
Stop. Drinking. With idiots. //

Outrage

Outrage. Disgust at lack of outrage. Get your rage out there quick-fire. Like like like love sad face. Outrage. Discuss his lack of outrage. Her squeamish response. Their privileged take. Check yours. Caveat endlessly.

As a white-cis-het-white-cis-het-prof-white-cis-het-prof of white-cis-het stuff I AM. And as I AM I AM outraged. Disgusted at your lack of outrage. Anger at angry troll logic actively searched for in the first place. The world is dreadful. The world is a muffin and white-cis-het-males lie atop it eating all the blueberries.

Excuse me, that's not quite accurate; not nuanced enou –

HOW WOULD YOU KNOW? I see the crumbs round your mouth, slurper. Outrage. Disgust at your lack of outrage. Calls for nuance and calm damned because fear slipped palpitations into hearts that want justice but aren't sure what they have, now. Bitterly spitting out pips they don't want – I am a white-cis-het-male and I am completely lost. But I AM. And as I AM I AM outraged. Disgusted by your lack of outrage. See you sitting there in the dark fumbling for a light-switch. Only a blue screen shines light for most now. Negligible knowledge of histories thwacked across every newsfeed. I add to that with a click. Full knowledge of my lack of some. I know nothing about how to stop this.

I know nothing

except that I have to believe in a better world even if I have to live in this one. ☹

Plural

i can't fail to project an i into the we
jigsaw snap a piece of my picture
into sore spot

can't fail to jolt
dumb fear at worst and
vitriolic angst at best
at this connection
to
poles ripping insides outside her for fun
acid flung in the face of her her and her and
her spine snapped after back lashed
for loving another her and
when she fought back her
eyes gouged out and
when she fought back her
face stomped
and all of those hers
killed at birth
fucked like pie
closer to home perhaps
college-student PornHub upload
rape
fetish drunk
her moaning low
rape
and
'rough sex' pardons for brute
murder of her
of us
of we
of her
of me and
list goes on, ad infinitum

collated
commemorated
1 in 5
2 per week
80% of
1 in 3 says

it is these folds and ridges and tunnels and
tubes and walls and cells and eggs
and caverns and unresearched secretive
whole of us
 – reduced to mere holes and
vacuums by those with
hatred in the bones of them at worst
ignorance at best – which
creates this us

i don't pretend answers
but know
where not to find them

Zero Fucks
ten vignettes in bereavement

1)

I'd like to go out on the ludicrous
from my wee slice of forever, but
I overheard there was something
else I should be giving, other
than forgiveness – elusive
hummingbird, so that creature is.

2)

I think I have concluded
but then there's a tumour
in the works, a spanner
in the dishwasher,
a baby sorely in need
of a bathtub – and then
there's this repeated action:
I keep pulling this weird
fork first from the drawer
despite having my late
grandmother's 12 piece
cutlery set in there, which
I love
12:1.

3)

How once upon a time we all are...

To pen this is despicable, but
I could've loved you more than
working you like a building
site – as long as possible but
with no blueprints.

4)

The ice caps melt in a gin and tonic.
I want for nothing, but just next-day-delivery
ordered a flamingo-patterned shower curtain,
spent the night so far
caps-locking my protest at
something or other and
binge-watching *Buffy*. Fuck it.
Bring it on. Get it done.
Stake it tae fuck.

5)

I mentioned three skeletons
but all are flesh tonight
and all were missed
before the missing
became permanent.

I will never find them for this.
I have the emotional range of a
human. Am not some kind of gerbil.
Just stop asking. I think I can
bear this, but not without guilt
flesh, goose-bumps, a spooky
pushing at the edge of things,
wanting them back,
all of them, as I've always done,
and now, though they never met,
all of em, they're swirling around
this room tonight, this kitchen
that none of them ever visited
til now. This night.

Next episode is the one
where Buffy slays the uber-vamp.

6)

Ye cannae destroy the base
but I've never had the patience
for precision. Never known
the correct distance or
what is appropriate –
death and I were always
a casual relationship.

7)

If you can pinch an inch
You can lose an inch!
Ah, Jenny, ye were becoming a wee bit
of a baw-face – glad ye've lost a bit!
Yer looking smashin.

My grandmother taught me
far more than this.
Yet this is what tonight brings,
is it? She meant chubby, by the way.
Not an actual baw-heid.

8)

Grief in the outskirts.
Queen of the overshare.
Queen of the fiery lash.
Queen of the bitten knuckle.
And yet I didn't reply.
I didn't reply to him.
Grief in the outskirts.

9)

Some will miss us.
It's not ok. None of this is.
They may be delicious, but
I will never again give them.
And I will never again think
I am incapable of loving.
Because that's what this is,
ultimately, this thrumming,
this distracting from what
needs now to occur – to be
gone through, to be lived.

10)

Thank you. Yes.
I will miss them, yes
and always.

Lighter

Being with her was like a game
 – a candle between us on the table:
the trick to quick swish an index finger
through the flame –
and this led to
laughter, cries of *Do it again! Do it again!*
sometimes, *Ooh yah bastard!* – a game
infectious, her encouragement risky, selfish,
addictive. But it never lasted.

Sometimes I found myself staring at an unlit stub.
Sometimes, too many times, she disregarded
the safe word, held my palm in til it blistered.
Eventually, too much knocking over of
the bastard thing in my direction –
I'd schlep home, morosely picking wax off
yet another formerly favourite cardigan.

There is regret in this,
as I eye the wax-stained table, because
at times we made good light.
But sometimes that kind of love will
burn you and your fucken house down
til there's nothing left to consume.

So. That Tuesday I left the matches at home.
She had stolen my lighter, of course.
It wasn't working for her anymore.

Ruff Ruff!

for B.

rrrrruuuuuff ruff luv!
u full up unstrung such bursts!
flux such tumults!
such lush lust rush-ups!
yum, cunny lucks pump numb – uh mmh!
much trustful fun – uh-huh – but
CLUTCH PLUM-PUD PLUMP RUMP!
mmmmmnnnn – HUH – uh – HUH –
uhhhh-huuuH-UH-h – mmmnnnnnb-b-b-bzzzzzz...

punch-drunk, slump snugly
pull rug up
just hug
mmmnnnnnnnn...   ...

ruff ruff
bubbly ruff ruff
cuddly curl up
snuffly gush-gush
yummy mm-hmms murmur
us
     us
         us...
luv?
YUP.

Take Off to Mid-flight Somewhere Across the Atlantic

I have to trust the other humans know what they're doing,
that all of these lights presumably mean something,
and that they knew what they were doing
when they invented this craft,
this way to traverse the largely unknowable...

Cos I sure as hell don't.
And I'm minding
that *Flight* movie with Denzel Washington.
Are we ten minutes to go from the need for
a stunning manoeuvre?
Can we survive this without a pilot fucked up
on cocaine and vodka?

I have to trust that lady who's passing chewy sweets to children
who are oblivious to death yet – have to trust I will not
    explode with
my last breath spent inhaling the scent of Tennent's
from the sweat of the gent beside me...

                              (is he sweating in fear though?
                                should I make a last friend?)

I have to trust that my own sweating palms
will grasp something future – other than these arm rests –
like his hands, his, him, oh fucken, HIS –
as they did last morning when our
bodies joyed rockingly to choiceful turbulence.

Dear Death, don't take me now, for I have
just discovered how to fly this –
as if gravity were nothing,
as if the emptiness were not waiting.

THERE COULD BE SO MUCH IMMINENT DEATH!

But across the aisle, that lad's already snoozing.
An announcement to place orders for baguettes
with the cabin crew almost assured me we might
survive this for bread and mayonnaise and
future heartburn –

BUT JOLT ME NOOOOOOO

Surely someone else is feeling this, is thinking this?
Thinking on the vastness?

This vastness that one just
leapt into
with surety of last breath last moon
last hug last swim last float last meal
last walk last time last gulp last beat
last jolt last step last time
last time last choice – was it
this vastness stole his love from him? –
last moon last tiny shine
 – he saw that below, christ –
jumped, stepped, leapt
no knowing
what's most accurate

thinking on the vastness not as he did, no – no
cos that way lies
that way lies – no no no love no

last tiny change
last huge shine

and I do never want to think in past last ways, no no –
I used to survive barely hiding but trying to
drown such thoughts –

but I'm for hat-tipping the vastness as long as I can now, thanks,
since I discovered this audible present
this hum of life

And these other humans – fellows in craft!
They're defiantly ordering cheese-and-ham croissants
and coffee that tastes like plastic shit and
milking tubes splashily into non-recyclable cups.

And I am high on fear and wine gums,
praying to deities I've never met,
trying to trust that other humans know
how all of this works.

See there – in front – a woman happily, curiously,
reading a crime novel!
I wonder what will be recovered from the wreckage after
the inevitable deep dive, these breaths...

GOD
jolts through me... 1...2...3...4...
exhale
GOD

I love living.
I want to survive so very much.
I don't know that I knew this until this very minute

as I fill up full of helplessness and love
and trust that there's machines that
do god's work, or
whatever the hell we'll call this.
This flight path I have to trust
makes total sense, though I
can't make heads nor tails of it,
nor shaky flimsy wings of it.

And I think I will always want this
plus another verse, and

I think it is love that makes this sadness and
that makes the sadness bearable.

Read Only

this 'I'
is Read Only
do not impinge with   word verb adjective
material thoughts   textbooks   boring cunt
fertiliser   hope love   adverbs
punctuation   dictionary definitions
sensible line breaks

> (let me skedaddle for this un
>   FFS – warned ye...)

don't assume pronouns
don't add ink squiggles

> (you absolute fascist)

this 'I' is Read Only
can't be added to by owt but editor
but it will be shared with you
via Instagram and endless Twitter threads
and butbutbut only mine to accept
create   express   say   you read only
with no comments but up-thumb
re-share niceness validate my heart-pump
throb emoji engine
plus a serious amount of malbec

P.S.: Love you folx. RTs welcome, thx. xxx

Notes

The poem 'This Script' was first commissioned for the Return Flight project of Melbourne-based lit mag *Going Down Swinging*. It was subsequently published in 404 Ink's 'The F Word' edition (Summer 2017).

'How to be a Stalker' is composed of direct quotes from three correspondents.

Acknowledgements

I would like to sincerely thank James T. Harding and Charlie Roy at Stewed Rhubarb for supporting and publishing this collection. Their vision for spoken-word poetry in print is a massive boon not only to my own, but many others work in Scotland and I am so grateful to them for their belief in my work.

For inspiring me out of the worst writer's block I have ever had in my puff, huge thanks to Caroline Bird, Magi Gibson and Luke Wright – the latter of whom introduced me to univocal poetry, which kick-started this entire collection. An extra thanks to Magi for providing exceptional editorial assistance on this collection. I could not have produced this work without her support, guidance, mentoring and her help with playing wi wurds on the page as fulsomely as I try to on the stage.

Thanks also to David Greig for his support of my work more broadly, and to Sonnet Youth for providing a stage to try out a great deal of this work in performance for the first time. Also, while ye can insert yer ain soundtrack, I wrote much of this while listening to RM Hubbert, Jonnie Common and Kathryn Joseph. So thank you for the tunes!

This collection is in part a complement to my stage-show and film-poetry project of the same name. For that I would like to thank Creative Scotland for the funds to collaborate with film-makers Perry Jonnson and Kevin McLean; composer/producers Audrey Tait and Lauren Gilmour (Novasound Studio); song-maker/producer Biff Smith and A New International, and director Jen McGregor. This support from Creative Scotland also enabled me the uninterrupted time I needed to focus on writing this book and I am hugely grateful for that.

Personal thanks go to the team at Flint & Pitch – Josephine Sillars, Chris Scott, Sian Bevan and Cameron Foster – for always having my back and for helping Make Hings Happen! For friendship, love and support, many thanks to Hannah Lavery, Kirsty Law, Laura Eaton-Lewis, Claire Stewart, Ma, Paw, Scott and Karen Lindsay. Huge gratitude to my grandfather, Archie Finlayson, for providing me with a space to write outwith Scotland for a fortnight, the flight to which led to the penultimate poem in this collection.

Finally, thank you to B for the flying missions, despite a mutual fear of heights. xxx

Lightning Source UK Ltd.
Milton Keynes UK
UKHW020246110419
340808UK00009B/93/P